D0327065

ARCIMBOLDO

T&J

This edition published 2011

Published by
TAJ BOOKS INTERNATIONAL LLP
27 Ferndown Gardens
Cobham
Surrey
KT11 2BH
UK
www.tajbooks.com

All notations of errors or omissions (author inquiries, permissions) concerning the content of this book should be addressed to info@tajbooks.com.

ISBN: 978-1-84406-170-9

ARCIMBOLDO

BY SANDRA FORTY

One of the most bizarrely creative artists to emerge during the High Renaissance is the Italian artist Giuseppe Arcimboldo who painted extraordinary portraits using vegetables, fruits, flowers, plant roots, wild animals and various other creatures, and natural objects. He started as a generic artist working on religious projects then moved on to conventional portraiture that apparently spontaneously blossomed into exotic eccentricity. Arcimboldo's paintings are full of puns and jokes and allegorical meanings that would have been easy for his contemporary Renaissance audience to interpret and enjoy but these meanings are lost on later generations.

Although Arcimboldo is known to have been a prolific artist, only around twenty of his paintings are still known to exist. He is an artist who became famous and celebrated within his lifetime but almost entirely disappeared from public consciousness after his death and the end of the Renaissance. He remained an obscure footnote painter for centuries, during which time many of his paintings disappeared: it is possible that there are many unattributed pre-assemblage Arcimboldo portraits lurking in collections and museums around Europe. His genius was rediscovered centuries later by the Surrealist artists working in the 1930s, since when his work has been appreciated for its unique originality and extraordinary qualities.

Arcimboldo started his professional career as a conventional religious artist, one of many Renaissance painters earning a reasonable living in the churches and courts of Europe. But these early works have long since been overlooked for his far more original and fantastical organic paintings that even in his lifetime earned him an original reputation and much admiration. Perhaps it was to ease the tedium that Arcimboldo started to elaborate his work with extraordinary and original imaginings and create his still life portraits; it has been speculated that he was inspired in part by Leonardo da Vinci's "grotesques." These paintings lie in somewhat strange ground half way between still lives and portraiture and although in modern times his work has been linked to the Symbolist movement, Arcimboldo is most often is labeled as a Mannerist in style.

Some critics view Arcimboldo's strange organic works as the product of an unbalanced mind, but most scholars categorise his work as fitting into the Renaissance tradition of celebrating the bizarre with their fascination with riddles, allegories, and puzzles of all kinds. This, in the context of the Renaissance, makes Arcimboldo an opportunist artist with a keen eye for the elitist tastes of his time.

Giuseppe Arcimboldo (also spelled Arcimboldi) was born in 1527 in the northern Italian city of Milan into a noble family of clergymen and artists of southern German ancestry. His mother was Chiara Parisi and his father Biagio Arcimboldo, an artist who worked for the office of the Fabbrica in the Great Duomo (Milan cathedral):

Giuseppe Arcimboldo and Giuseppe Meda, The Jesse Tree, fresco, 1556, Monza, Cathedral

his grandfather and other relatives had been Archbishops of Milan. As he was growing up he was surrounded by all the glory, extravagance, and imagination of the High Renaissance. Little is known about his early life except that it was probably one of privilege and access to the significant members of Milanese society and all the important visitors, artists, scholars, and writers who spent time in the city.

The greatest Milanese artist of all was Leonardo da Vinci who died in France in 1519, but he left his notes and sketchbooks behind in Milan with one of his pupils, Bernardino Luini. Luini's son knew Arcimboldo and showed him the priceless notebooks which must have influenced the young man with their skill, imagination, and sheer breadth of knowledge.

In 1549 when he was 22, Arcimboldo started working in the glass workshops of the Duomo with his father when they were commissioned to design stained-glass windows for the cathedral. His only identified work concerns the stories of St. Catherine of Alexandria in 48 parts that they started together, but he finished alone after his father died in about 1551. Arcimboldo continued to work for the Duomo designing stained-glass windows after his father's death, and Duomo records show that he was paid for designing other windows without stating which ones, although experts can detect his distinctive elements in some. Significantly, in 1551 Ferdinand of Bohemia (later Emperor Ferdinand I) was staying in Milan and commissioned Arcimboldo to paint

Cathedral in Milan, Italy. Scenes from the life of Saint Catherine of Alexandria, Stained glass window above the entrance of the right-hand transept, drawn by Biagio Arcimboldi and Giuseppe Arcimboldi, made by Corrado de' Mochis (1556).

five coats of arms for him; eleven years later he was to become Arcimboldo's patron in Vienna.

In 1556 Arcimboldo was working with Giuseppe Meda on the frescoes for the Cathedral of Monza, although he was still primarily working for the Duomo. In 1558 he drew the cartoon for a large Gobelin tapestry entitled the "Dormition of the Virgin Mary" that still hangs in Como Cathedral near seven similar, but unattributed, sumptuously floral tapestries dating from around the same time. All are of the same size and feature many of the same decorative elements. These are almost certainly designed by Arcimboldo, but no authentication has been found.

The Holy Roman Emperor Ferdinand I was so taken with Arcimboldo's work that he repeatedly petitioned him to come and work for him. Eventually, in 1562, Arcimboldo agreed and took the prestigious and well remunerated position of royal painter (court portraitist) at the Imperial Hapsburg Court in Vienna, a position he was to retain for 26 years. Arcimboldo's first assignment was to make several royal portraits and during the same period he made the first of his Four Seasons paintings (c. 1563): he was then aged about 36 and a mature painter in full command of his medium.

In July 1564 Emperor Ferdinand I died and was succeeded by Emperor Maximilian II who retained Arcimboldo's services as court painter at a salary of 20 guilders a month (plus bonuses when the emperor was particularly pleased). Various written

sources indicate Arcimboldo was painting all the time but details are scarce and few pictures survive from this period, however, to help with his workload he took on an assistant, Giambattista Fonteo.

Some of his extant works from this time are the series of *The Four Elements* (1566): this comprises four individual paintings: *Water* (made up from fish and other aquatic animals), *Fire* (made from canon, fire arms, spills, flint, and flames), *Earth* (a collection of animals including a lion and an elephant), and *Air* (made up from many different species of bird—in particular the Hapsburg symbols of the eagle and the peacock). Another work from 1566 is *The Lawyer* (aka *The Jurist*) who has a face composed of amphibians, fish, and meat and a torso composed of books. The accompanying painting of *The Librarian* (1566) shows a man made entirely of books in allusion to his profession. For New Year 1659 Arcimboldo gave his patron Maximilian *The Four Seasons* and *The Elements* accompanied by a poem composed by himself and his assistant Fonteo.

Arcimboldo returned to another series of *The Four Seasons* in 1572, then two more complete series the following year, with one of the sets commissioned by Maximilian as a gift for the Prince Elector of Saxony. He is also known to have painted *The Cook* (one of his upside-down paintings) and *The Wine Steward* in 1574. When King Augustus of Saxony visited the Viennese court in 1570–1573, he saw and admired Arcimboldo's work and commissioned

him to make a copy of his *The Four Seasons* but this time incorporating his own royal symbols.

Arcimboldo established a good personal relationship with all three emperors and it is reported that he was popular at court and was held in such esteem that he would be granted permission to see Emperor Maximilian at any hour of the day. He is known to have made some paintings for the emperor's private chambers in 1575 for which he was given 75 thalers, but any other works he made at this time have disappeared. Emperor Maximilian gave Arcimboldo a special and final gift of 200 guilders in 1576, probably in recognition and thanks for all his hard work, and in addition officially recognized Arcimboldo's illegitimate son Benedict (though

nothing else is known about him or his circumstances).

In October 1576 Emperor Maximilian died and his son Emperor Rudolph II succeeded and retained Arcimboldo as court painter. The next eleven years appear to have been Arcimboldo's most prolific period during which he established a close relationship with the eccentric and introverted new emperor who trusted him completely as his artistic advisor, architect, spectacle planner, designer, and friend.

Arcimboldo was also court costume designer and decorator and imperial party planner for the glittering gala events so beloved by the Imperial court—especially the great tournaments and feasts, lavish affairs attended by important dignitaries,

religious officials, visiting heads of state, and other significant people. These occasions were not just lavish entertainments, they were more importantly emphatic statements about the power and wealth of the House of Hapsburg as the pre-eminent power in Europe. As their brilliant architect, choreographer, and designer Arcimboldo was himself a man of considerable influence and power.

Although they were regular events at the Hapsburg court and Arcimboldo was their principal planner, he is only documented as organizing two festivals (although he almost certainly contributed to many more including that of the wedding in Prague of Elizabeth, daughter of Maximilian II, to Charles IX of France in 1570). He designed, choreographed, and orchestrated the wedding feast of Archduke Charles II of Austria to Maria Anna of Bavaria in August 1571 in Vienna. Another spectacular was the coronation of Rudolph as King of Hungary in 1572 (he became Emperor Rudolph II in 1576).

For the spectaculars Arcimboldo invented many original special effects, perhaps most notably his "Harpsichord of Color" a huge water-driven musical instrument. He became noted for his illusionist trickery and other effects included rivers of champagne, gilded fountains, flocks of vividly colored birds, and elaborate parades which on one famous occasion had horses disguised as dragons and a real-life elephant.

When he wasn't designing elaborate court entertainments Arcimboldo

was required to undertake numerous royal portraits of the imperial family and other important heads of state; many of these portraits also required duplicates as well. His strange paintings rapidly found an enthusiastic audience and such still-life portraits became the rage. Perhaps to keep himself interested Arcimboldo made a further elaboration of portraiture with the occasional inverted illusion portrait: what appears to be an ordinary bowl of fruit, for example, when turned upside down becomes a bizarre portrait instead.

In about 1575 Arcimboldo made a small pen and ink self-portrait. It shows an unsentimental drawing of a scholarly looking bearded man in late middle age. It is the only known likeness of him although he possibly inserted his features into his last painting in 1590. In 1580 Emperor Rudolph confirmed Arcimboldo's noble status and allowed him to upgrade his coat of arms.

Two years later, in 1582 Emperor Rudolph, a sufferer of chronic bouts of depression, moved his court to Prague to escape the rigors of Vienna; Arcimboldo and his assistant Fonteo moved with him. Rudolph's court attracted all the great European scholars and scientists, such as the German mathematician and astronomer Johannes Kepler and Tycho Brahe, the Danish astronomer and alchemist—as well as many great painters and poets.

In parallel to the intellectualism of the court and to sate his intellectual hunger, the emperor commissioned

Arcimboldo to research and buy interesting natural curiosities, animals, and works of art. He is recorded as having traveled to Kempten in southern Germany in 1582 where he bought birds and various strange objects from the New World. These the emperor collected into a cabinet of curiosities that had earlier been expanded by his father (with the help of Arcimboldo) and which later grew into The Art and Wonder Chambers. This contained all manner of strange and exotic things: stuffed birds, animals and strange fish, giant mussel shells, mummies, unusual gemstones, rare objects from far away places, and even demons imprisoned in blocks of glass; plus, of course, an accompanying zoo of exotic animals. By now a trusted and close friend, Arcimboldo had the unique privilege of being able to study in close detail all these unusual and peculiar items and often made nature studies of them that he almost certainly used as reference material for his composite paintings. Many of these studies were so accurate that they are believed to have been acquired for his own collection by the eminent Bolognese naturalist Ulisse Aldrovandi.

1585 is the last known time that Arcimboldo painted any pictures at court, but that year he dedicated a red leather-bound folio containing 148 blue pen and ink drawings of costumes, decorative items and headgear, of animals fantastical and real to Emperor Rudolph—"The Invincible Emperor of the Romans His Everlasting and most Benevolent Sovereign and Majesty

Rudolph II by Giuseppe Arcimboldo of Milan: sundry different ideas designed by his own hand for the furnishing of tournaments. In the Year of Our Lord 1585."

Arcimboldo stayed at court for a further two years but any works he made have not been recorded. By now he desperately wanted to return home, perhaps feeling his age and fearing the Emperor's deteriorating mental and physical state. But despite repeated requests he did not get permission to leave until 1587 by which time he had completed eleven years' service to Emperor Rudolph and 26 years' service to the Imperial Hapsburg court altogether. Arcimboldo at last got permission to return home to Milan— but on condition that he still painted for the Emperor when requested. As a

parting gift for his "long, faithful and conscientious service" he was given 1,500 Rhenish guilders.

On returning home to Milan Arcimboldo set up a studio and worked on producing a composite portrait of Rudolph II (later titled *Vertumnus*) and started *Four Seasons in One Head*. In 1591 he produced two of his most famous and celebrated paintings, *Flora the Nymph* and *Vertumnus* that he sent to the emperor in Prague. The latter is the ancient god of vegetation and transformation of the seasons, and Arcimboldo gave him the face of Emperor Rudolph. He also wrote a poem about Vertumnus that owed a lot to an earlier poem by the Roman poet Sextus Propertius, in particular they both list seasonal flowers, fruits, and vegetables which then appear in the same order from top to bottom in the painting. The painting alludes to the fact that Emperor Rudolph rules over the seasons and elements and that along with the animals, all things live in harmony and peace under his benign rule.

The emperor was delighted with his portrait and rewarded Arcimboldo in 1592 with one of his highest honors. However, the painting was one of the trophies looted by the Swedish army in 1648 and is now on display in Skokloster Castle in Sweden.

In about 1590 Arcimboldo produced his last masterpiece, *Four Seasons in One Head*, which is possibly a self-portrait of himself in old age. The following year the poet and theologian Gregorio Comanini described the painting in his treatise *Il Figino overo delfine della Pittura*: (On the Purpose of Painting: Art Theory in the Late Renaissance):

"... A knotty tree trunk forms the chest and the head in which certain cavities serve as mouth and eyes and a protruding knob as the nose. Knots covered with moss form the beard, and some branches in front form the horns. This stump, stripped of its own leaves and fruit, represents Winter, which produces nothing but enjoys what is produced by other seasons. Some flowers placed on the breast and over the shoulder signify Spring. Summer is represented by bundles of wheat and a few attached twigs, a straw cloak that covers the shoulders, two cherries hanging from a branch that forms the ear, and two plums arranged behind the head. Autumn is represented by two bunches of grapes, one white and one red, hanging from a branch, and by some apples showing among green ivy branches that spring from the top of the head. One of the branches of the head has been peeled slightly from around the middle, and the little scraps of bark curl back from the white part which is inscribed Arcimboldus.P. . . "

Translated and edited by Ann Doyle-Anderson and Giancarlo Maiorino, 2001.

On July 11 1593, aged about 66, Arcimboldo died in Milan. His entry in the death register at the Magistro della Sanita records the cause of death as "retention of urine and kidney stones."

Many art historians believe that the work of Arcimboldo had a profound influence on his contemporary Caravaggio. But after his death and the end of the Renaissance Arcimboldo's paintings were largely forgotten and almost completely overlooked and many of his paintings disappeared altogether.

In 1648 during the Thirty Years' War when the Swedish army invaded and sacked Prague many of Arcimboldo's paintings were looted from Rudolf II's art collection on the orders of Queen Christina of Sweden and taken back to Sweden for her collection—which accounts for the unexpected occurrence of a number of his painting in the far north.

For three hundred years or so Arcimboldo's remaining paintings hung unremarked and often dirty at the back of art collections in Vienna and Sweden and it was not until the

twentieth century Surrealists in the
1930s, in particular Salvador Dali,
took an interest in his work that the
first modern study appeared. Benno
Geiger published a detailed analysis of
his known works in 1954 and a general
reassessment of Arcimboldo's work
started. Many of his pictures came out
from their dark corners and benefited
from a careful restoration before being
put out on fresh display.

UNDERSTANDING THE PAINTINGS

Arcimboldo's educated Renaissance contemporaries delighted in discovering and interpreting the many symbols and allusions he made in his paintings, meanings that imparted so much more than is apparent to a casual viewer. For one thing he often painted his extraordinary assemblage pictures in series of four, such as the Elements and the Seasons—the latter a favorite subject he returned to many times—and set them as contrasts to each other, for example young–old, earth–air or wet–fiery. Furthermore, contemporary Renaissance understanding of nature was closely bound up with the gods and goddesses of the ancient world and many of the portraits encompass both nature and myth. Layer on further astrological, spiritual, and imperial facets and the paintings become even

more densely embroidered in meaning; additionally their ultimate intention was to celebrate the greater glory of the emperor, Arcimboldo's employer. It is also believed that the emperors he worked for then passed on a number of these paintings as gifts to subtly reinforce the reality of the power of the House of Hapsburg to the recipient and their followers.

Giambattista Fonteo, who became Arcimboldo's assistant in Vienna, was himself a prolific poet and writer. He shed light on his master's works when he described their complexity, comparing the Seasons and Elements and explaining that they share the same properties: "Summer is hot and dry like fire, winter is cold and wet like water, both the air and spring are hot and wet, and autumn and the earth are cold and dry." Additionally Arcimboldo's work was celebrated by many of his contemporaries in writing and poetry.

Another important component of Arcimboldo's work is that his fruits and vegetables, flowers, insects, and birds are all highly detailed depictions of the real thing: the only imagination is in the way he assembled the elements, not in the elements themselves. A valuable research tool for this was Emperor Rudolph's collection of curiosities that he had free rein to study and understand. Ultimately many of the curiosities became incorporated into his paintings. Almost always painting to commission, Arcimboldo would occasionally indicate his patron (most often the Emperor) by subtly incorporating his coat of arms into the composition.

The Four Seasons paintings were a popular subject Arcimboldo frequently returned to. He tended to make the Spring portrait a young woman composed of fresh flowers. Summer was an older but still attractive woman made up from ripe fruit. Fall was a mature man assembled from fall fruits; Winter an elderly and wizened man composed of roots, leaves, and branches. These were portraits painted symmetrically in profile as a set, with the first face pointing left, the second right, then left and finally right. Always intended to delight and amuse, Arcimboldo devised a variation on the assemblage portraits: he would paint an apparently ordinary bowl of fruits and flowers, which if turned 180 degrees became a face.

CHRONOLOGY OF ARCIMBOLDO'S LIFE

1527 Birth of Giuseppe Arcimboldo in Milan. His mother's name is Chiara Parisi. His father is Biagio Arcimboldo, a painter. Birth of Maximilian II.

1549 24 December: first mention of Arcimboldo's name in the register of the workshop at Milan Cathedral, where he is working as one of his father's assistants.

1552 Birth of Rudolph II, son of Maximilian II.

1558 Arcimboldo finishes his work at Milan Cathedral. Designs for a gobelin tapestry for Como Cathedral.

1562 Arcimboldo moves to Vienna, where he is appointed to the court as a portrait artist and copyist. Maximilian is crowned King of Bohemia and of the Roman Empire.

1563 Arcimboldo paints his first series of Seasons.

1564 Maximilian becomes Holy Roman Emperor.

1565 Arcimboldo is named in the Imperial court register as the court taker of likenesses.

1566 Arcimboldo paints The Lawyer and begins his series of The Four Elements. Travels to Italy.

1568 Giambattista Fonteo becomes Arcimboldo's assistant.

1569 Maximilian is given the Seasons and Four Elements at New Year. Arcimboldo and Fonteo write a poem to accompany the paintings.

1570 Maximilian II's daughter Elizabeth marries Charles IX of France and a grand festival is put on in Prague. Arcimboldo is one of the organizers and participants.

1571 Archduke Charles of Austria marries Maria of Bavaria in Vienna, and Arcimboldo, together with Fonteo and Jacopo Strada, takes charge of the organization.

1572 Copies of the Seasons.

1573 Arcimboldo paints the third and fourth versions of the Seasons, which Maximilian II has ordered as a gift of homage to the Prince Elector of Saxony.

1575 Rudolph II is crowned King of Bohemia in Prague, and shortly afterwards King of the Roman Empire in Regensburg.

1576 Death of Emperor Maximilian II, Rudolph II becomes Emperor.

1580 Rudolph II ennobles the Arcimboldo family.

1584 G. Lomazzo's commentary on Arcimboldo, the first on the artist, is published in Lomazzo's Trattato dell' Antichita della Pittura.

1585 Arcimboldo makes Rudolph II a present of 148 designs for costumes, headgear and decorative wear.

1587 Arcimboldo leaves Prague and goes to Milan. The Emperor gives the artist 1550 guilders in recognition of his services.

1589 Arcimboldo sends his Flora from Milan to Prague. It is accompanied by a poem by Gregorio Comanini.

1591 Comanini publishes Il Figino in Mantua. Arcimboldo's portrait of Rudolph II as Vertumnus is sent to Prague with a poem by Comanini.

1592 Paolo Morigia's Historia dell' Antichita di Milano is published in Venice.

1593 Giuseppe Arcimboldo dies in Milan.

Plate 1

BIRTH OF ST. CATHERINE

1551; 45.6 x 26.3 inch (116 × 67 cm); Stained Glass
Milan Cathedral, pane #6 on the 14th window of the S. Apse

Plate 2

ST. CATHERINE TALKS TO THE EMPEROR ABOUT THE TRUE FAITH

1551; 45.6 x 26.3 inch (116 × 67 cm); Stained Glass
Milan Cathedral, pane #57 of the 14th window of the S. Apse

Plate 3

PEASANT WOMAN GOING TO MARKET

1560; 10 x 7.1 inch (25.5 x 18.1 cm); Pen and brush on heavy paper
Biblioteca Nacionale, Madrid

Plate 4

THE PASSING OF THE VIRGIN
1562; 166.5 x 185 inch (423 × 470 cm); mural tapestry
Como Cathedral, Como, Italy

Plate 5

TREE OF JESSE
ca. 1562; Fresco
Monza Cathedral, Lombardy

THE SPRING 1563

1563; 25.9 x 19.6 inch (66 x 50 cm); Oil on Oakwood
Museo de la Academia de Bellas, Madrid Spain

Plate 6

Plate 7

THE SUMMER 1563
1563; 33 x 22.4 inch (84 × 57 cm); Oil on limewood
Kunsthistorisches Museum, Vienna

Plate 8

WINTER 1563
*1563; 26.2 x 19.8 inch (66.6 x 50.5 cm); Oil on lime wood
Kunsthistorisches Museum, Viena, Austria*

Plate 9

HOLY ROMAN EMPEROR MAXIMILIAN II. OF AUSTRIA
AND HIS WIFE INFANTA MARIA OF SPAIN WITH THEIR CHILDREN

ca. 1563; 94.8 x 74 inch (240 x 188 cm)
Schloss Ambras Innsbruck

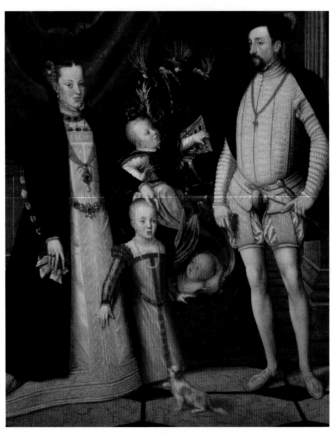

Plate 10

THE LAWYER

1566; 25.2 x 20 inch (64 × 51 cm); oil on canvas
Statens Konstsamlingar Gripsholm Slott Stockholm, Sweden

39

Plate 11

THE FIRE
1566; 26.2 x 20 inch (66.5 x 50.8 cm); Oil on Wood
Vienna, Kunsthistorisches Museum

Plate 12

WATER
1566; 26.3 x 20.5 inch (67 × 52 cm); Oil on limewood
Kunsthistorisches Museum, Gemäldegalerie, Vienna

Plate 13

EARTH

1566; 27.6 x 19.2 inch (70.2 x 48.7 cm); Oil on Wood
Private Collection, Austria

Plate 14

AIR
1566; 29.5 x 22 inch (75 x 56 cm); Oil on canvas
Private Collection, Basel, Switzerland

Plate 15

EARTH 1570
1570; 27.6 x 19.2 inch (70.2 x 48.7 cm); Oil on Wood
Private Collection Vienna Austria

Plate 16

THE DINNER
1570; 20.4 x 16.1 inch (52 × 41 cm); oil on canvas
Private collection Stockholm, Sweden

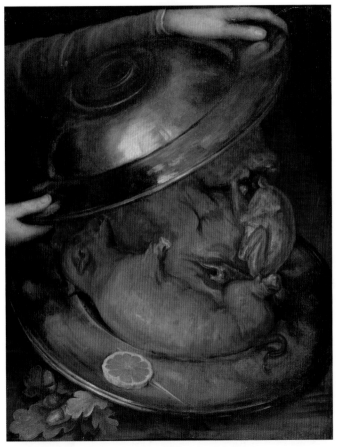

Plate 17

THE COOK (THE DINNER REVERSED)

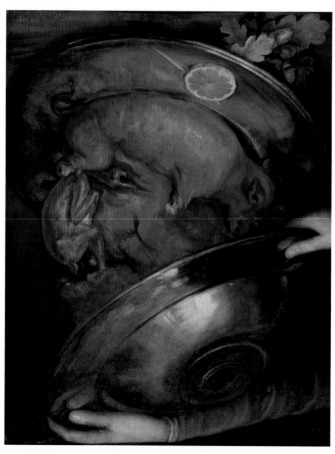

Plate 18

THE LIBRARIAN
1570; 38.1 x 27.9 inch (97 × 71 cm); Oil on canvas
Skokloster Castle Stokholm, Sweden

Plate 19

COSTUME FOR CERBERUS
1571; 9.8 x 7.4 inch (25 × 19 cm); blue ink on paper
Uffizi, Florence, Italy

Plate 20

COSTUME FOR CHARON
1571; 9.8 x 7.4 inch (25 × 19 cm); blue ink on paper
Uffizi, Florence, Italy

Plate 21

COSTUME FOR GEOMETRY

1571; 15.3 x 7.8 inch (39 × 20 cm); blue ink on paper
Ufizzi, Florence, Italy

Plate 22

COSTUME FOR MUSICK
1571; 11.8 x 7.8 inch (30 × 20 cm); blue ink on paper
Ufizzi, Florence, Italy

Plate 23

SPRING 1572

1572; 30.1 x 24.4 inch (76.6 x 57 cm); Oil on canvas
Private collection, Bergamo

Plate 24

SUMMER 1572
1572; 29.4 x 22.2 inch (74.7 x 56.5 cm); Oil on canvas
Private collection, Bergamo

Plate 25

THE AUTUMN 1572

1572; 36.5 x 28.2 inch (92.71 x 71.76 cm); Oil on Canvas
Private Collection, USA (on loan to Art Museum, Denver).

Plate 26

WINTER 1572

1572; 30.2 x 22.3 inch (76.8 x 56.7 cm); Oil on canvas
Private collection, Bergamo

Plate 27

WATER
1572; Size Unknown; Oil on Panel
Private Collection

Plate 28

SPRING 1573
1573; 29.9 x 25.2 inch (76 x 64 cm); Oil on canvas
Musee National du Louvre, Paris Frane.

Plate 29

SUMMER 1573
1573; 29.9 x 25.2 inch (76 x 64 cm); Oil on canvas
Musee National du Louvre, Paris Frane.

Plate 30

AUTUMN 1573
1573; 29.9 x 25.2 inch (76 x 64 cm); Oil on canvas
Musee National du Louvre, Paris Frane.

Plate 31

WINTER 1573

1573; 29.9 x 25.2 inch (76 x 64 cm); Oil on canvas
Musee National du Louvre, Paris Frane.

Plate 32

ADAM

1578; 16.9 x 13.9 inch (43 x 35.5 cm); Oil on Canvas
Private collection Basel, Switzerland

Plate 33

EVE AND THE APPLE

1578; 16.9 x 13.9 inch (43 x 35.5 cm); Oil on Canvas
Private collection Basel, Switzerland

Plate 34

HEAD WITH FRUIT BASKET
1590; 22 x 16.3 inch (55.9 x 41.6 cm); Oil on wood
French & Company LLC, New York

Plate 35

HEAD WITH FRUIT BASKET (REVERSED VIEW)

Plate 36

THE FOUR SEASONS

1590; 23.7 x 17.5 inch (60.4 x 44.7 cm); Oil on poplar
Private Collection, New York

Plate 37

VERTUMNUS (PORTRAIT OF RUDOLF II)

1590; 27.7 x 22.6 inch (70.5 x 57.5 cm); Oil on panel.
Skoklosters Slott, Stockholm

Plate 38

THE VEGETABLE GARDENER

1590; 13.7 x 9.4 inch (35 x 24 cm); Oil on Wood
Museo Civico Ala Ponzone, Cremona, Italy

Plate 39

THE VEGETABLE GARDENER (REVERSED VIEW)

Plate 40

FLORA
1591; 28.7 x 22 inch (73 x 56 cm); Oil on panel
Private Collection Paris

Plate 41

THE ADMIRAL
Date and Size Unknown; Oil on Panel
Private Collection

Plate 42

THE LADY OF GOOD TASTE
Date and Size Unknown; Oil on Panel
Private Collection

Plate 43

WHIMSICAL PORTRAIT
Date and Size Unknown; Oil on Panel
Private Collection

Plate 44

DESIGN OF A SLEDGE
Date Unknown; 7.4 x 9 inch (19 x 23 cm); Blue pen-and-wash on paper

Plate 45

DRAWING OF AN ELEPHANT
Date Unknown; 9.4 x 7.3 inch (24 x 18.7 cm); Ink on paper

Plate 46

DESIGN OF A COSTUME FOR "RHETORICK"
Date Unknown; 11.8 x 7.8 inch (30 x 20 cm); Blue pen-and-wash on paper

Plate 47

DESIGN OF A COSTUME FOR "ASTROLOGY"
1571; 11.8 x 7.8 inch (30 x 20 cm); Blue pen-and-wash on paper

Plate 48

DISEÑO DE UN TRINEO
Date and Size Unknown; Blue pen-and-wash on paper

Plate 49

PROCESSING OF SERICULTURE
Date and Size Unknown; Blue pen-and-wash on paper

Plate 50

PROCESSING OF SERICULTURE 1
Date and Size Unknown; Blue pen-and-wash on paper

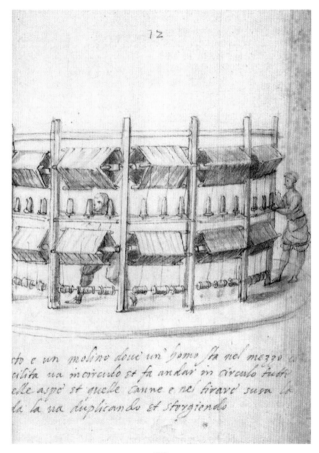

Plate 53

PROCESSING OF SERICULTURE 4
Date and Size Unknown; Blue pen-and-wash on paper

. qui la maestra mette dentro a una gran' Caldan
piena d'agua calda le galle et quella alton te
mena l'aspa et ua tirandi su la seda su filzou

Plate 54

PROCESSING OF SERICULTURE 5
Date and Size Unknown; Blue pen-and-wash on paper

come la galla e fatta le femine le cauano da
rami della Genestra et le metten' al sole ac
detto figatto mora dentro alla Galla perchò
torna a nasere perchè come la galla o fuorata
e piu buona per far la seda

Plate 55

PROCESSING OF SERICULTURE 6
Date and Size Unknown; Blue pen-and-wash on paper

Dapoi che detto bigatto e fatto alla grossezza che
di essere le femine uano mboschando cō ra
de Genestra saluatica et bigatto ua per le ra
facendo la gala

Plate 56

PROCESSING OF SERICULTURE 7
Date and Size Unknown; Blue pen-and-wash on paper

qui si coglie la foglia del moro bianoho per p...
detti figatti

Plate 57

PROCESSING OF SERICULTURE 8
Date and Size Unknown; Blue pen-and-wash on paper

Plate 58

PROCESSING OF SERICULTURE 9
Date and Size Unknown; Blue pen-and-wash on paper

Plate 59

THE SENSE OF SMELL
Date Unknown; 28.2 x 36.0 inch (72 x 92 cm); Oil on Panel
Southampton City Art Gallery, UK

Plate 60

THE SEASONS 1
Date Unknown; 37 x 28.7 inch (94 x 73 cm); Oil on canvas
Private collection

Plate 61

THE SEASONS 2
Date Unknown; 37 x 28.7 inch (94 x 73 cm); Oil on canvas
Private collection

Plate 62

THE SEASONS 3
Date Unknown; 37 x 28.7 inch (94 x 73 cm); Oil on canvas
Private collection

Plate 63

THE SEASONS 4

Date Unknown; 37 x 28.7 inch (94 x 73 cm); Oil on canvas
Private collection

Plate 64

SUMMER
Date Unknown; 29.9 x 25 inch (75.9 x 63.5 cm); Oil on Canvas
Private Collection

Plate 65

WINTER
Date Unknown; 29.9 x 25 inch (75.9 x 63.5 cm); Oil on Canvas
Private Collection

Plate 66

HEROD

Date Unknown; 17.9 x 13.4 inch (45.6 x 34 cm); Oil on canvas
Tiroler Landesmuseum Ferdinandeum, Innsbruck, Austria